MJ COLE

Touring Italy on a Budget

Discover the easiest, most cost-effective ways to experience the many splendors of Rome, Florence, Venice, and more.

Contents

1

Introduction

Welcome to Touring Italy on a Budget travel guidebook. I am so excited to be creating this book for you. The primary reason I decided to write this book was so that I could share the absolute joy and love I have of the many fascinating wonders I have experienced from my time living and touring Italy.

I have a couple of true things I love to do and experience, and when I combine all three in one place or trip, how cool is that? Those things are food, wine, history, and travel. Italy brings all these things to life, and honestly, I've not experienced another locale that has met all those marks in one place.

How have I come to this conclusion? I served more than 20 years in the U.S. Navy, and through that career, I was blessed to be able to travel the world. I have been around the globe several times and have walked on every continent on the face of the planet, with one exception, Antarctica, but there's still time. Anyhow, in those travels, I have visited more than forty countries. Now that I've retired from the naval service, I travel for fun, food, history, and wine.

I've had the good fortune to live all over the world, including many locations in the U.S., including Hawaii, and overseas in Afghanistan and Italy. Other than the U.S., Italy is where I have lived for the most extended period. I've come to love the people, food, history, and wines that Italy has to offer.

So why this book? Travel is a passion for many, but in many cases is cost-prohibitive. Well, I'm here to tell you that a 10-day trip to Italy can happen for less than you might expect. There are several keys to making this a reality; planning, researching, and knowing what you truly want to get from your time and money on the trip. That is why this book will focus heavily on pre-trip planning. Additionally, pre-trip planning will save you time and money in Italy and help you build and sustain excitement for your trip. The downside is that you'll likely find so much more that you want to do that you'll have to make tough decisions about how you will fit into your first trip.

What we'll cover in this book.

- Pre-trip planning
- Arrival and getting settled.
- Familiarization
- Moving about
- Favorites in Rome, Venice, and Florence
- Helpful tips and tricks along the way
- Helpful words and phrases
- And a few not-so-well-known Must-See's

This book is based on a recent trip I made with the family to Italy, where our original entry point was Venice, and our second primary location was Rome. There were many great adventures in between, but for ease of reading and continuity, we'll walk through this trip. So, let's get into it, and please enjoy.

I recommend several companies in this book, but please know that I have no financial stake or financial interest in any of them. These are just the ones I have found to be the most economical and rewarding.

2

Pre-Trip Planning

Some may think that pre-trip planning isn't much more than finding a flight, a hotel, and maybe a rental car, but like anything in life, failure to plan is a plan destined to fail. Having lived in Italy for several years and having made multiple trips with family back to Italy, I can tell you with complete confidence that planning saves money, time, and, most importantly, stress. Travel can be extremely stressful, but it doesn't have to be. Planning, knowing where to be, when to be, how to get there, and what you'll need when you arrive saves money, time, and headaches.

What does pre-trip planning look like?

- Dates: how many days do you have to plan for?
- How many hotel nights do you have to book?
- How many days can you spend in the locations you want to see? (more on this later)
- Research – this is critical.
- What is most important to you to see and do on this trip?

- What are your "Must-See" stops?
- If Rome is top on the list, then flights are easy to figure out.
- If it's a multiple-city trip, other flight planning will be needed.
- More on this later.
- Ground Transportation
- We'll get into more detail on this in a little bit.
- Communication and technology
- Day-Trips – a great way to see a lot more at a reasonable cost.
- Restaurants

Research

When traveling to Italy, there are a few key things to remember. For starters, August is generally the Italian vacation month. I would not recommend August as the time to visit Italy.

Weather:

Weather is a significant factor. Are you a mild Spring Day type of person, or more a crisp Fall type of person? My favorite times to travel in Italy range from September through October or May and June. Now granted, these are peak travel times for most people, but there's a reason for that. The temperatures are warm enough not to require big, bulky coats and such yet mild enough that you have to be concerned about sweating your tail off.

What will you see?

Now that your dates are picked out, what can you reasonably fit into that schedule? One great thing about Italy is that rail, metro, and taxis are plentiful and generally easy to figure out. So, it is reasonable to spend several days in one major city, then take the train to the next major city, therefore maximizing every hour while there.

With your departure date and return home date, it's time to look for flights.

Here's an example of one 10-day itinerary starting from the U.S. we've recently taken:

- Overnight flight to Venice's Marco Polo Airport
- Most all U.S.-based departures are overnight flights to Italy.
- Arrive in Venice at 9:00 AM the following day (count this as day 1)
- Spend two nights in Venice.
- Depart day three after lunch.
- Rapid train from Venice to Rome in the afternoon of day three, roughly 3 hours.
- We took the rapid train for the experience and comfort.
- Arrive at Rome Termini around dinner time.
- Booked for eight nights.
- This is where day trips are a real advantage (more on that later).
- -Day 10 – plenty of time, so no rush. Check out of the hotel and take the train to Leonardo Davinci Airport for an afternoon departure home.

Of course, this is very simplified, but in the planning stages, it's important to know arrivals and departures, and then it's time to fill in the gaps with those "Must See" things that are the whole reason for the trip. We could have broken up this itinerary and spent a night or two in Florence but given our "Must See" list for this trip; we decided to head straight to Rome.

Research the major things you absolutely must see while in Italy and make a list. Here are some examples based on our 10-day trip noted above.

Venice

- Murano Glass Artisans
- Burano
- Saint Mark's Basilica
- Saint Mark's Square
- Rialto Bridge

Rome

- The Vatican, Sistine Chapel, St. Peter's Basilica
- Colosseum
- The Roman Forum
- Trevi Fountain
- Circus Maximus
- Trastevere
- The Roman Ghetto

Of course, there are so many more things to see and do in either of these cities, but these are offered to aid you in researching your "Must See" list. Don't worry; as you continue researching and find new and wonderful things to add to the list, you can update as you go.

Now that you have your departure and return dates, your entry and departure cities, and a solid "Must See" list, it's time to start filling in the blanks.

Day Trips

Day trips offer an incredibly affordable and simple way to see so much more in a shorter period than if you try to do this on your own. There are many vendors for these day trips; my favorite is City Wonders (www.citywonders.com).

Day trips from most major cities in Italy are a great way to make your travels easier. Consider if you want to travel on your own to Venice, Florence, Tuscany, Pisa, Caserta, Pompei, Vesuvius, Amalfi, and Positano. In total, you'd be looking at maybe eight or nine days, most of which would be consumed by getting to each of these locations, checking in and out of multiple hotels, packing and unpacking, and dragging luggage all over Italy. Why would anyone subject themselves to such toils?

In the example trip noted earlier, we were able to check into and out of only two hotels, lug our full suitcases between only two cities, and see nearly all of the places listed using day trips. When you consider the cost of moving from city to city, taxis and other transportation, the expended time and hassles of dragging luggage around, day tips make all the sense in the world. Granted, some of the day trips are very long days, but they are well worth it.

So, as you do your research, check out day trips from your launch points, and see how they could work into your schedule. Ensure you're keeping your notes and resources handy; you'll need them once you've laid out your plan.

Ground Transportation

The wonders of the internet and all the information at your fingertips are indeed your best friend. One of the biggest headaches with traveling to an unfamiliar city is getting around. Good for you that you have this book to help you research this critical topic ahead of time. I will continue to use the example trip noted previously as a reference point in transportation options in Italy, but the concept applies to any city in Italy.

Our first transportation challenge after arriving in Italy was how do we get from the airport to Venice proper. A little research discovered that there are five ways to make this trip.

Bus

ATVO Bus (my favorite choice)

- This is the express bus, meaning no stops in between.
- Tickets are purchased at the arrival terminal at the airport.
- Buses queue up just outside the airport arrivals exit.
- The cost is less than ten euros one way.
- The trip is about 25 minutes.
- Departs every 30 minutes.

ACTV Bus

- Same as the ATVO bus, but it is more of a "city bus" and takes a little longer.

- The cost is only slightly less than the ATVO.

Water Bus
  -Alilaguna

- The cost is about 15 euros one way.
- The trip takes about an hour and fifteen minutes.
- There are three lines Red, Blue and Orange, depending on where you want to end up in Venice.

If you want the whole tourist experience, this may be an option but not one I recommend.

Water Taxi
  -The most expensive option runs anywhere from 100 euros to 150 euros.
  -For a large group, this could be a viable option.

Train
  -This is possible, but not one that is reasonable from the airport, since you would first have to catch a bus from the airport to the train station.

Taxi
  -Indeed, an option and at about 45 euros, if you don't want to wait on the bus, this is a reasonable option.

The buses and regular taxis will deposit you at the Piazzale Roma, and as there are no roads in Venice, you'll either walk or catch a water taxi from here to the nearest drop-off point for your hotel. We'll get into hotel choices next.

Wherever you are in Italy, transportation options are many. I focused on Venice above as an example of the various available options. The research applies to whatever city you will be traveling to. A little planning will make your time in Italy that much more fulfilling. When I get to the section about Rome, I'll add a transportation section specific to Rome because there are some essential things to know and understand before you get there.

Choosing Your Hotels

There are so many personal desires for hotels that it would be nearly impossible to cover all the choices in this short guide. So, we'll focus on some of the top considerations I've found to be the most effective for ease of transportation, coupled with the level of sophistication and comfort I look for in hotel choices.

If you think about it, the hotel is not a place you will be spending a great deal of time other than sleeping and resting for your next day's adventures. Sure, it has to have the basics and be comfortable, Wi-Fi is a given, and it would be nice if it had a small bar or café for a meeting in the morning or winding down each night, but that's about it. The great thing about Italy, in most cities, hotels are plentiful and can be found near the rail stations.

The number one concern for me in choosing a hotel is the ease of access from the major transportation hubs for my trip. Since my trips generally depend on using rail, metro, and my own two feet to get around, I tend to choose hotels close to the train terminals or, in the case of Venice, close to the central bus drop-off point. Let's face it, dragging a fifty-pound suitcase around town is not fun.

Another key consideration, and a mistake I've made to my own detriment, is if the hotel has an elevator.I know this may sound silly, but considering most hotels in Italy are in buildings-built hundreds of years ago, it's not a guarantee that they will have an elevator. So, if you don't want to lug that same fifty-pound suitcase up several flights of stairs, confirming that your hotel of choice has an elevator is a good idea.

I am a big fan of Hotels.com. Sure, you could find a slightly lower price on other travel sites, but I have found that this site offers all the critical information on many hotels in one place, making it easy to compare hotels before making your choice. Also, with their rewards program, you can earn free nights through this site, so why not!

Communication and Tech

This is a short but essential part of pre-trip planning.

Most cellular service carriers offer a reasonable rate for international data and calling plans. For example, Verizon offers a Travel Pass for $10 daily on days used. Of course, high-speed data usage caps out at 2GB, and data flow rates are reduced after that, but they offer more high-speed data once you've hit that limit. This is an essential tool for many reasons; Google Maps is one, and access to metro apps is another. Not to mention, I used my cell phone to research restaurants quite often.

Most, if not all, hotels offer free Wi-Fi, which will help keep your data usage in check but having that access while exploring is a very nice tool to have at your disposal. Not to mention you can also text all those who didn't make the trip and make them wish they were there with you.

Other options exist if your cellular carrier does not offer an international travel package. International sim cards can be purchased online before travel, depending on whether your device will accept the international sim card. There are also sites like Cellular Abroad (www.cellularabroad). These plans vary greatly, so research is key.

Of course, you can always depend on Wi-Fi; know beforehand that this option will limit your accessibility and mobility. I've traveled to Italy with and without cellular service. To be quite candid, I only used cellular service on my last trip because of the inexpensive option through my cellular provider.

Another key thing you will need in Italy is an adapter for the electrical outlets. These can be found easily on Amazon. You won't need any special transformer, just an outlet adapter. One item that could also come in handy is a small rechargeable power cell, again easily found on Amazon; just be sure it has a standard outlet charging cord since USB charging ports are not widely available.

3

You're in Italy Now – Venice

The Grand Canal is a journey of architectural marvels, and cultural splendor.

I f you're looking for a magical place to explore and travel to, then Venice, Italy, is a great option. Located in the Veneto region in Northern Italy, this historic city is full of unique landmarks and breathtaking scenery. From the picturesque Grand Canal and romantic gondolas to the iconic Saint Mark's Basilica, there is so much to explore in this enchanting city.

One of the most popular attractions in Venice is the Grand Canal. This iconic body of water is lined with beautiful buildings and bridges, making it the perfect place to take a romantic gondola ride. As you float past the stunning Venetian architecture, you'll have the chance to get a close look at the charming city.

Another must-visit destination in Venice is Saint Mark's Basilica. This incredible building is nothing short of spectacular. With its grand facade, colorful mosaics, and Venetian art, it's worth a visit. This place is the epicenter of Venice and is crowded with locals and tourists alike. Plus, the impressive interior is home to the world-famous Pala d'Oro, one of the most dazzling religious artifacts in the world. And it's an excellent place for people-watching.

Take a day trip to Murano and watch masters create elegant glass pieces.

If you're looking to get off the beaten path, then the neighboring islands of Murano, Burano, and Torcello are perfect for an excursion. Murano is known for its glass-blowing factories, with colorful and unique glass pieces on display. Burano is a quiet fishing village with brightly painted houses, while Torcello is home to ancient Byzantine mosaics.

Murano Glass: An Artisan's Masterpiece

Murano glass has been a symbol of craftsmanship and elegance for centuries. This luxurious material has been a coveted resource for the wealthy elite for ages, and its beauty and grace have been unparalleled by any other art form.

The history of Murano glass can be traced back to the 13th century when artisans in the Italian city of Murano began to specialize in glass making. By the 16th century, Murano had become the main center of glass production. During this period, Murano glass was so coveted that it was even used as currency. Its production remained a closely guarded secret, allowing the artisans of Murano to maintain their dominance in glass production.

Murano glass is made in a variety of forms and shapes, and it comes in a range of colors and patterns that make it stand out among glass products. It is made with a variety of techniques, including blowing, casting, and pressing, and each artisan chooses their own unique style. Murano glass is known for its intricate patterns, thin layers, and vibrant colors. It is also very durable due to the special formulas used in its production.

The unique properties of Murano glass make it a coveted material for artisans to work with. Its elegance and beauty have been admired for centuries, often seen in sculptures, jewelry, and other decorative pieces. Whether it's glowing in the sunlight or casting its reflections on the walls, Murano glass always displays a level of craftsmanship that is unparalleled by any other glass product.

Murano glass is truly a timeless and beautiful material, and its craftsmanship is something to be admired. Its history and beauty make Murano glass the ultimate symbol of luxury, and it will never cease to be a source of admiration.

While one of my favorites is learning the history of such places as Murano, Venice is so much more.

The floating city of Venice is an unparalleled place, filled with a rich history, cultural significance, and beauty. As many know, it is a city comprised of islands, each with its unique character and charm.

The city of Dorsoduro, for example, boasts some of the world's most incredible galleries and art museums, displaying world-class collections from all over the globe. Not far, Cannaregio is a neighborhood filled with delicious seafood restaurants offering a plethora of flavors to please any palate.

But Venice isn't just about the sights. It's a city of depth and culture, with many traditions, customs, and celebrations. From the Carnevale to the Venetian Arts Biennale, the city celebrates its unique identity in a way few others can rival.

There are no streets in Venice. The many canals are their streets.

The locals are friendly and passionate, and they take great pride in their city. You can hear the echoes of their stories and life experiences as you stroll through the narrow alleyways and canals, taking in the sights and sounds of Venice. And the city's rich history is evident in the architecture, artwork, and monuments that can be found around every corner.

It's a magical place, like something out of a fairytale. But it's much more than that. It's a city full of life, love, and laughter, a place with a spirit and soul that's impossible to ignore. Visit once, and you'll feel like you've been there for a lifetime.

There's something special about Venice that truly sets it apart from the rest. It's a city with an undeniable charm that won't soon be forgotten.

So, make sure to add this magical city to your travel list and prepare to be dazzled!

4

On to Rome - The Eternal City

Rome, the Eternal City, is a timeless place that has stood at the crossroads of world history, art, culture, and civilization. From the ancient ruins of the Forum Romanum, the Pantheon, and Circus Maximus, to the grandeur of St. Peter's Basilica, the Vatican, and the Sistine Chapel, Rome is a living history museum for all to explore.

Rome is a symbol of the power and greatness of the Roman Empire, and its legacy can be seen throughout the city. The city is known for its impressive monuments, landmarks, and historical sites, all offering insight into the past and present. From the Colosseum, a remnant of gladiatorial contests, to the Trevi Fountain, one of the most stunning fountains in the world, to the Spanish Steps, the most famous staircase in the world, Rome is filled with breathtaking sights and experiences.

Traveling around Rome is easy with its well-connected metro system and regular bus routes. The city is well laid out, with a host of unique neighborhoods and attractions to explore. For the food and wine enthusiast, Rome is famous for its delicious pizzas, pastas, and locally produced wines.

Insider Tip

Rome has a myriad of hop-on-hop-off bus tours. Don't overlook this feature as a tool for gaining an excellent overall understanding of the city and to help orient yourself to this marvelous city. For a very little sum, you can purchase an all-day pass, and as the name implies, jump on and off as you learn from the host all the city's marvels. I recommend doing this as soon as you can because it will hit all the highlights, and the narrated tour will help you over the coming days as you fine-tune your itinerary. As you're on the bus, keep an eye out for the Metro stops, their signs are easy to pick out and will help you navigate as you explore.

Metro signs are easy to spot and will be a key navigation beacon.

Rome is an ideal destination for travelers seeking a unique mix of modern and ancient of culture, history, and tradition. The city is a living testament to the power and breadth of the Roman Empire and its many contributions to modern life, from its foundational role in legal and democratic governance structures to its awe-inspiring art, culture, and artifacts. For anyone looking to travel to Rome, the Eternal City awaits to dazzle and delight.

Ah, Rome, the eternal city, is a place that is steeped in history, culture, and delicious food. As a traveler to Rome, with so many things to do and see, it can be overwhelming. But planning will ease this feeling.

The entrance to the Vatican Museum, where all the tours begin for the Vatican and Sistine Chapel.

First and foremost, the historical sites. Rome is home to some of the most iconic sites in the world. From The Vatican, with its impressive St. Peter's Basilica and St. Peter's Square, to the

Sistine Chapel and its breathtaking ceiling, followed by the Trevi Fountain, the Spanish Steps, the Colosseum, and finally, Piazza Navona, it's hard to pick which is the best of these.

The food in Rome is outstanding. With delicious pasta dishes and Italian wines, you'll be sure to enjoy your meals here. Plus, Rome offers some of the best gelato in the world, so don't forget to save room for dessert!

Another bonus of visiting Rome is its easy metro service. The Metro is a great way to get around the city, and it goes to all of the historical sites. Plus, you can find metro cards that offer discounts on sites and attractions, so be sure to pick one up before you go.

The metro system in Rome is one of my favorites. A network of underground rail stations, and the hub, Roma Termini, make this a truly magnificent way to get around in Rome. Travelers can purchase day passes for about five euros or multi-day passes for slightly more. The metro maps are easy to understand, and the line information boards on the trains alleviate any concerns about missing your stop. This is why I always pick a hotel within easy walking distance to the Roma Termini, so my daily travels around Rome all center to and from this easily accessible rail hub.

Day Trips

We've already discussed day trips, but Rome is my favorite jumping-off point for day trips. Whether you purchase a motorcoach-style day trip or venture off on your own, either can easily be accomplished from Rome. Visit a 16th-century winery in Tuscany, coach on down to the Amalfi coast, or motor on up to Florence; day trips from Rome are hands down the most cost-effective and travel-easy ways to see Italy.

16th Century wine cellar in Montepulciano, in the Tuscany region of Italy.

An easy and exciting day trip away from Rome. Montepulciano is the home of the world-renowned Brunello Wines. You can also purchase these famous wines, cheeses, and balsamic vinegar and have it shipped straight to you your home.

Insider Tip Day Trip

A great day trip you can do on your own is to the city of Caserta and the Royal Palace and Gardens. An easy train trip from Rome Termini to Caserta is affordable and simple. Take a morning train to Caserta, visit the Royal Palace and Gardens, and you can be back in Rome by dinner.

An easy day trip from Rome, the Royal Palace, and Gardens of Caserta are a Must-See.

The Royal Gardens of Caserta, located just outside of Naples in southern Italy, is a breathtakingly beautiful and grandiose destination that holds a special place in royal and regal history. Built to rival the famous gardens of Versailles, these gardens are some of the largest and most elaborate in Europe and have served as a backdrop for films, documentaries, and music videos.

Designed by the Italian architect Luigi Vanvitelli in the 1700s, these gardens are an Italian answer to the French garden designs of the time. Spanning over 2.5 miles, The Royal Gardens of Caserta feature over 200 statues, ornate fountains, and vast terraces that frame the natural beauty of the rolling hills, lakes, trees, and views of Mt. Vesuvius.

In the center of these gardens lies the Palace of Caserta, a breathtaking example of Baroque architecture and a must-see for anyone visiting the area. Spread across 4,000 hectares, the palace is one of the largest in the world, and its various courtyards, gardens, and artworks throughout the palace make it a stunning place to explore.

At the heart of the gardens is the Reggia di Caserta, a stunning 18th-century palace and park that was built for the Bourbon family. One of the most visited landmarks in the area, the royal palace and its gardens are a testament to the pomp and grandeur of Italian architecture and the power of the Bourbon family.

The Royal Gardens of Caserta are a stunning reminder of the grandeur of Italian architecture and the power of the Bourbon family in centuries past. With its sweeping vistas, ornate fountains, and grand statues, the gardens are a beautiful and majestic place to explore and experience a piece of Italian history.

All in all, Rome is an amazing place to visit. With its historical sites, delicious food and wine, and easy metro service, it's definitely worth the trip. Enjoy your time in the eternal city!

5

Florence - The Renaissance City

Michelangelo's David

F lorence is one of those cities in Italy that you can spend a day or a week in. It's truly up to your "Must See" list. Easily accessible by train from Venice or Rome or on a day trip from either city, there are many options to fit Florence into your itinerary.

Florence is a city that never ceases to amaze. Sitting at the heart of the Tuscany region of Italy, it is an ancient city that has seen incredible things over the centuries. From being a major trading center at the dawn of the Middle Ages to the birthplace of the Renaissance and of some of the most iconic pieces of art this world has ever seen, Florence is a city steeped in history and culture.

The Florentine dialect is spoken throughout the city and the surrounding area, and the locals have a strong sense of pride in their language and culture. It's no surprise that the city is a UNESCO World Heritage Site, and it's easy to see why when you wander through its streets.

One of the world's most iconic pieces of art, Michelangelo's David, is located in Florence, and it's definitely worth a visit. Other stunning sculptures in the city include the four statues of the Medici Chapel by Michelangelo and the marble statue of Perseus by Benvenuto Cellini, both of which can be found in the Accademia Gallery in Florence.

The city is also home to two of the most influential writers in human history, Dante Alighieri and Niccolo Machiavelli, both of whom lived in Florence during their lifetimes and were influential in shaping both the literary and political history of the city. For literary fans, the city offers a true treasure trove of delights.

Whether you're looking for a culturally enriching experience or you want to explore the stunning sights and sounds of one of the most fascinating cities in Europe, a trip to Florence is sure to be an unforgettable experience.

Florence is a city where a visitor could spend a day or a week. It's truly a Must-See city. Florence is easily accessible from Venice or Rome by train but is also a common day trip from either city as well. I prefer making Florence a day trip for ease of travel and cost. However, one day, I will make Florence a hub city from which I can travel more readily to more of Tuscany.

The Duomo

From the towering Duomo di Firenze to the stunning Ponte Vecchio, Florence is a city of timeless beauty and history. But this isn't just a place to marvel at the past; it's a vibrant city full of world-renowned culture, cuisine, and entertainment. Florence is a must-see if you're looking for the ultimate travel experience.

The best part about visiting Florence is its ease of getting around. Its compact size and well-maintained public transportation make it easy to get to any part of the city needed. The hills and cobblestone streets of the city are best explored on foot, and Locanda della Margherita, the best hotel in Florence, offers the perfect starting point.

When it comes to dining, Florence is at the absolute top of its game. Its world-class restaurants offer everything from local Tuscan cuisine to the finest Italian dishes. Be sure to sample the original pizza, or some delicious Italian wines, both easily found in the city's vast array of eateries.

And of course, no trip to Florence is complete without exploring the city's rich history. The fabulous works of Michelangelo, Dante and Botticelli, among others, can be found all around the city, from the Uffizi Gallery and Palazzo Vecchio to the Santa Croce and the Piazza della Signoria.

Whether you're there for the food, the wine, the sights, or to soak up the Renaissance atmosphere, Florence is a must-see travel destination. You won't be disappointed, from its vibrant culture and delicious cuisine to its stunning architecture and rich history. So make sure to add Florence to your list of places to visit and experience it for yourself.

6

Other Must-See Day Trips

I f you're looking to explore the beauty of Italy, you've come to the right place. From the stunning Amalfi coastline to the majestic royal rooms of the Palazzo Reale di Caserta and the volcanic wonders of Vesuvius, Italy offers travelers a full gamut of activities and cultural explorations.

The beach at Positano.

Start your journey in the romantic seaside village of Positano, situated along a stunning stretch of the Amalfi Coast. This ancient town is surrounded by awe-inspiring cliffs and the vibrant shades of the deep blue sea and offers breathtaking panoramic views. From the crystal clear waters of the Tyrrhenian and Ligurian Seas to the unique Mediterranean cuisine and nightlife, Positano has something for everyone.

Continue your Italian adventure by visiting the walled city of Montepulciano. This charming medieval hill town is a great place to explore history and art, and sample some of the region's finest wines. As your journey takes you further south, you'll come to the majestic Royal Palace and Gardens of Caserta. This breathtaking residence of the kings of Naples and Sicily was designed by Vanvitelli and is an absolute must-see!

16th Century winery at Montepulciano.

No visit to Italy is not complete without a trip to Pompeii and a hike up the nearby Vesuvius. This Mediterranean volcano is an incredible sight to behold - its limestone cliffs, cinder cones, and steaming vents of magma all provide a striking backdrop to its ancient ruins.

Of course, no visit to Italy would be complete without its wonderful cuisine. From cheesy pizzas and creamy pastas to the traditional limoncello and granita, travelers can find something for every palate.

With its unrivaled beauty and abundance of cultural attractions, Italy is a fantastic destination for travelers. From the serene views of the Amalfi Coast to the royal palace of Caserta, from the local cuisine to the achingly perfect vistas of Vesuvius, Italy awaits your discovery.

7

Conclussion

O bviously, there are so many fascinating sites and wonders in Italy that it would take multiple volumes to speak to them all. Prior planning, though, will help you focus in on what's truly important to you and maximize your visit while keeping on budget. There are many resources to help you in your trip planning and research, some of which you'll find in the resources section of this guide.

You'll notice we never discussed rental cars in this guide because, quite frankly, it's too easy to use other modes of transportation in and around Italy, and unless you genuinely want to get off the beaten path, you won't need a rental car.

I do hope that this guide will inspire you to take that trip you've always dreamed of, and help you make that trip with confidence.

If you like this guide and it helped you build your dream trip, please leave a review on Amazon.

Buona giornata e buon viaggio

8

Words and Phrases

G ood day and happy travels.

  • Buona giornata e buon viaggio

  Where can I buy a train ticket?

  • Dove posso comprare un biglietto del treno? (swap treno with metro for the metro)

Where is the bathroom?

  • Dov'è il bagno?

Thank you.

  • Grazie

Good morning

- Buongiorno

Good evening

- Buonasera

Good night

- Buonanotte

Excuse me

- Mi scusi

Where – Dove (pronounced doh-vay)

Buy or purchase – comprare (pronounced com-prar-eh)

Ticket – bigglietto (pronounced bill-yet-oh)

9

Resources

Wikipedia contributors. (2021, November 23). *Casertavecchia*. Wikipedia. https://en.wikipedia.org/wiki/Casertavecchia

Wikipedia contributors. (2023, February 13). *Paestum*. Wikipedia. https://en.wikipedia.org/wiki/Paestum

City Wonders. (n.d.). *Rome Tours - Colosseum, Vatican and Day Trips from Rome*. https://citywonders.com/rome-tours?

Wikipedia contributors. (2023b, February 22). *Herculaneum*. Wikipedia. https://en.wikipedia.org/wiki/Herculaneum

City Wonders. (n.d.-b). *Tuscany Day Trip from Rome: 3-Course Lunch and Wine Tasting Included*. https://citywonders.com/rome-tours/tuscany-day-trips-from-rome

Wikipedia contributors. (2023a, January 28). *Caserta*. Wikipedia. https://en.wikipedia.org/wiki/Caserta

Tripadvisor. (n.d.). *Lazio: Tours and Tickets*. https://www.tripadvisor. com/Attraction_Products-g187789-a_contentId.40944372647+7142 47328-Lazio.html

wanderwisdom.com. (n.d.). https://wanderwisdom.com/travel-destinat ions/How-to-get-from-Marco-Polo-Airport-to-Venice

International Travel Plans & Services - Verizon. (n.d.). https://www.ver izon.com/plans/international/international-travel/?cmp=KNC-C-M obility-NON-R-BPLU-NONE-NONE-2K0VZ0-COE-GAW-12392

Cellular and Data Plans for Italy. (n.d.). https://www.cellularabroad.co m/italy-phone-plans.php

Wecker, M. (2022, March 30). *Why Is Murano Glass So Special (and Expensive)? Experts Give Us 8 Reasons*. Artnet News. https://news.ar tnet.com/art-world/why-is-murano-glass-so-special-and-expensive-experts-give-us-8-reasons-2056030

No citation available
   https://www.getyourguide.com/-l32/

Printed in Great Britain
by Amazon

40947142R00030